The Wrong End of the Rainbow

Also by Charles Wright

POETRY

Buffalo Yoga (2004)

A Short History of the Shadow (2002)

Negative Blue (2000)

Appalachia (1998)

Black Zodiac (1997)

Chickamauga (1996)

The World of the Ten Thousand Things: Poems 1980–1990 (1990)

Zone Journals (1988)

The Other Side of the River (1984)

Country Music: Selected Early Poems (1983)

The Southern Cross (1980)

China Trace (1977)

Bloodlines (1975)

Hard Freight (1973)

Grave of the Right Hand (1970)

CRITICISM

Quarter Notes (1995)

Halflife (1988)

The Wrong End of the Rainbow

QUARTERNOTE CHAPBOOK SERIES #4
SARABANDE BOOKS
LOUISVILLE, KENTUCKY

POEMS CHARLES WRIGHT

Copyright © 2005 by Charles Wright

No part of this book may be reproduced without written permission of the publisher. Please direct inquiries to:

Managing Editor
Sarabande Books, Inc.
2234 Dundee Road, Suite 200
Louisville, KY 40205

Library of Congress Cataloging-in-Publication Data

Wright, Charles, 1935–
    The wrong end of the rainbow : poems / by Charles Wright. — 1st ed.
        p.   cm.
    ISBN 1-932511-12-1 (pbk. : alk. paper)
    I. Title.
    PS3573.R52W76 2005
    811'.54—dc22   2004010654

Cover and text design by Charles Casey Martin

Manufactured in the United States of America
This book is printed on acid-free paper.

Sarabande Books is a nonprofit literary organization.

Partial funding has been provided by the Kentucky Arts Council, a state agency in the Commerce Cabinet, with support from the National Endowment for the Arts.

FIRST EDITION

CONTENTS

APPALACHIAN FAREWELL

Sunset in Appalachia, bituminous bulwark
Against the western skydrop.
An Advent of gold and green, an Easter of ashes.

If night is our last address,
This is the place we moved from,
Backs on fire, our futures hard-edged and sure to arrive.

These are the towns our lives abandoned,
Wind in our faces,
The idea of incident like a box beside us on the Trailways' seat.

And where were we headed for?
The country of Narrative, that dark territory
Which spells out our stories in sentences, which gives them an end and
   beginning...

Goddess of Bad Roads and Inclement Weather, take down
Our names, remember us in the drip
And thaw of wintery mix, remember us when the light cools.

Help us never to get above our raising, help us
To hold hard to what was there,
Orebank and Reedy Creek, Surgoinsville down the line.

LAST SUPPER

I seem to have come to the end of something, but don't know what,
Full moon blood orange just over the top of the redbud tree.
Maundy Thursday tomorrow,
                              then Good Friday, then Easter in full drag,
Dogwood blossoms like little crosses
All down the street,
                    lilies and jonquils bowing their mitred heads.

Perhaps it's a sentimentality about such fey things,
But I don't think so. One knows
There is no end to the other world,
                              no matter where it is.
In the event, a reliquary evening for sure,
The bones in their tiny boxes, rosettes under glass.

Or maybe it's just the way the snow fell
                              a couple of days ago,
So white on the white snowdrops.
As our fathers were bold to tell us,
                        it's either eat or be eaten.
Spring in its starched bib,
Winter's cutlery in its hands. Cold grace. Slice and fork.

Inland Sea

Little windows of gold paste,
Long arm of the Archer high above.
Cross after cross on the lawn. Dry dreams. Leftover light.
Bitter the waters of memory,
Bitter their teeth and cold lips.

Better to stuff your heart with dead moss,
Better to empty your mouth of air
Remembering Babylon
Than to watch those waters rise
And fall, and to hear their suck and sigh.

Nostalgia arrives like a spring storm,
Looming and large with fine flash,
Dissolving like a disease then
                          into the furred horizon,
Whose waters have many doors,
Whose sky has a thousand panes of glass.

Nighttime still dogs and woos us
With tiny hiccups and tiny steps,
The constellations ignore our moans,
The tulip flames
                  snuffed in their dark cups,
No cries of holy, holy, holy.

Little windows of gold paste,

Long arm of the Archer high above.

Cross after cross on the lawn. Dry dreams. Leftover light.

Bitter the waters of memory,

Bitter their teeth and cold lips.

THE SILENT GENERATION II

We've told our story. We told it twice and took our lumps.
You'll find us here, of course, at the end of the last page,
Our signatures scratched in smoke.

Thunderstorms light us and roll on by.
Branches bend in the May wind,
But don't snap, the flowers bend and do snap, the grass gorps.

And then the unaltered gray,
Uncymbaled, undrumrolled, no notes to set the feet to music.
Still, we pull it up to our chins; it becomes our lives.

Garrulous, word-haunted, senescent,
Who knew we had so much to say, or tongue to say it?
The wind, I guess, who's heard it before, and crumples our pages.

And so we keep on, stiff lip, slack lip,
Hoping for words that are not impermanent—small words,
Out of the winds and the weather—that will not belie our names.

HIGH COUNTRY CANTICLE

The shroud has no pockets, the northern Italians say.
Let go, live your life,
                              the grave has no sunny corners—
Deadfall and windfall, the aphoristic undertow
Of high water, deep snow in the hills,
Everything's benediction, bright wingrush of grace.

Spring moves through the late May heat
                              as though someone were poling it.

THE WRONG END OF THE RAINBOW

It must have been Ischia, Forio d'Ischia.
Or Rome. The Pensione Margutta. Or Naples
Somewhere, on some dark side street in 1959

With What's-Her-Name, dear golden-haired What's-Her-Name. Or Yes-
    Of-Course
In Florence, in back of S. Maria Novella,
And later wherever the Carabinieri let us lurk.

Milano, with That's-The-One, two streets from the Bar Giamaica.
Venice and Come-On-Back,
                              three flights up,
Canal as black as an onyx, and twice as ground down.

Look, we were young then, and the world would sway to our sway.
We were riverrun, we were hawk's breath.
Heart's lid, we were center's heat at the center of things.

Remember us as we were, amigo,
And not as we are, stretched out at the wrong end of the rainbow,
Our feet in the clouds,
                              our heads in the small, still pulse-pause of age,

Gazing out of some window, still taking it all in,
Our arms around Memory,
Her full lips telling us just those things
                              she thinks we want to hear.

A SHORT HISTORY OF MY LIFE

Unlike Lao Tzu, conceived of a shooting star, it is said,
And carried inside his mother's womb
For sixty-two years, and born, it's said once again, with white hair,
I was born on a Sunday morning,

                         untouched by the heavens,
Some hair, no teeth, the shadows of twilight in my heart,
And a long way from the way.
Shiloh, the Civil War battleground, was just next door,
The Tennessee River soft shift at my head and feet.
The dun-colored buffalo, the sands of the desert,
Gatekeeper and characters,

                       were dragon years from then.

Like Dionysus, I was born for a second time.
From the flesh of Italy's left thigh, I emerged one January
Into a different world.

                It made a lot of sense,
Hidden away, as I had been, for almost a life.
And I entered it open-eyed, the wind in my ears,
The slake of honey and slow wine awake on my tongue.
Three years I stood in S. Zeno's doors,

                     and took, more Rome than Rome,
Whatever was offered me.
The snows of the Dolomites advanced to my footfalls.
The lemons of Lago di Garda fell to my hands.

Fast-forward some forty-five years,

                          and a third postpartum blue.

But where, as the poet asked, will you find it in history?

Alluding to something else.

Nowhere but here, my one and only, nowhere but here.

My ears and my sick senses seem pure with the sound of water.

I'm back, and it's lilac time,

The creeks running eastward unseen through the dank morning,

Beginning of June. No light on leaf,

No wind in the evergreens, no bow in the still-blonde grasses.

The world in its dark grace.

                      I have tried to record it.

THE SODBUSTER'S SALOON AND HALL OF FAME

Each time they knock one back,

                            another longhorn kneels in the dust.

Each time they settle up, another strand of barbed wire

Is stretched to the vanishing point,

                        that staked and stalled horizon.

Outside, their horse-and-wagons,

                        in slow motion toward paradise,

Turn west at the edge of town.

They take a loose rein, they take a deep seat

                        and give the horses their heads,

Dipped in their rodeo dreams:

                    Up next

Out of chute no. 1 on Upside Down, Amos Many Wounds,

His belt buckle big as the moon,

                and sharp-edged, and glistening like wire points in the sun.

A Field Guide to the Birds
of the Upper Yaak

A misty rain, no wind from the west,
Clouds close as smoke to the ground,

                             spring's fire, like a first love, now gone to ash,

The lives of angels beginning to end like porch lights turned off
From time zone to time zone,

                             our pictures still crooked on the walls,

Our prayer, like a Chinese emperor, always two lips away,
Our pockets gone dry and soft with lint.
Montana morning, a cold front ready to lay its ears back.

If I were a T'ang poet, someone would bid farewell
At this point, or pluck a lute string,

                             or knock on a hermit's door.

I'm not, and there's no one here.
The iconostasis of evergreens across the two creeks
Stands dark, unkissed and ungazed upon.
Tonight, it's true, the River of Heaven will cast its net of strung stars,
But that's just the usual stuff.

                    As I say, there's no one here.

In fact, there's almost never another soul around.
There are no secret lives up here,

                          it turns out, everything goes

Its own way, its only way,
Out in the open, unexamined, unput upon.
The great blue heron unfolds like a pterodactyl

Over the upper pond,

                        two robins roust a magpie,

Snipe snipe, the swallows wheel, and nobody gives a damn.

WAKING UP AFTER THE STORM

It's midnight. The cloud-glacier breaks up,
Thunder-step echoes off to the east,

                              and flashes like hoof sparks.
Someone on horseback leaving my dream.

Senseless to wonder who it might be, and what he took.
Senseless to rummage around in the light-blind stars.

                                       Already

The full moon is one eye too many.

IMAGES FROM THE KINGDOM OF THINGS

Sunlight is blowing westward across the unshadowed meadow,
Night, in its shallow puddles,

                          still liquid and loose in the trees.
The world is a desolate garden,
No distillation of downed grasses,

                    no stopping the clouds, coming at us one by one.

————

The snow crown on Mt. Henry is still white,

                         the old smoke watcher's tower
Left-leaning a bit in its odd angle to the world,
Abandoned, unusable.
Down here, in their green time, it's past noon

                and the lodgepole pines adjust their detonators.

————

The blanched bones of moonlight scatter across the meadow.
The song of the second creek, with its one note,

                     plays over and over.
How many word-warriors ever return

                  from midnight's waste and ruin?
Count out the bones, count out the grains in the yellow dust.

CONFESSIONS OF A SONG AND DANCE MAN

The wind is my music, the west wind, and cold water
In constant motion.
                    I have an ear
For such things, and the sound of the goatsucker at night.
And the click of twenty-two cents in my pants pocket
That sets my feet to twitching,
                              that clears space in my heart.

"We are nothing but footmen at the coach of language,
We open and close the door."
                            Hmmm two three, hmmm two three.
"Only the language is evergreen,
                        everything else is seasonal."
A little time step, a little back-down on the sacred harp.
"Language has many mothers, but only one father."

—————

The dying *narcissus poeticus* by the cabin door,
Bear grass, like Dante's souls,
                        flame-flicked throughout the understory,
The background humdrum of mist
Like a Chinese chant and character among the trees,
Like dancers wherever the wind comes on and lifts them . . .

The stillness of what's missing
                        after the interwork's gone,

A passing sand step, a slow glide and hush to the wings—
A little landscape's a dangerous thing, it seems,
Giving illusion then taking it back,

                          a sleight of hand tune
On a penny whistle, but holding the measure still, holding the time.

————————

A god-fearing agnostic,

                    I tend to look in the corners of things,
Those out-of-the-way places,
The half-dark and half-hidden,

                    the passed-by and over-looked,
Whenever I want to be sure I can't find something.
I go out of my way to face them and pin them down.

Are you there, Lord, I whisper,

                    knowing he's not around,
Mumble *kyrie eleison,* mumble O three-in-none.
Distant thunder of organ keys
In the fitful, unoccupied

                  cathedral of memory.
Under my acolyte's robes, a slip-step and glide, slip-step and a glide.

————————

Red-winged blackbird balancing back and forth on pond reed,
Back and forth then off then back again.
What is it he's after,

              wing-hinge yellow and orange,
What is it he needs down there
In snipe country, marsh-muddled,

                       rinsed in long-day sunlight?

The same thing I need up here, I guess,
A place to ruffle and strut,

                   a place to perch and sing.
I sit by the west window, the morning building its ruins
In increments, systematically, across the day's day.

Make my bed and light the light,

               I'll be home late tonight, blackbird, bye-bye.

AGAINST THE AMERICAN GRAIN

Stronger and stronger, the sunlight glues
The afternoon to its objects,

                     the baby pine tree,
The scapular shadow thrown over the pond and meadow grass,
The absence the two

                   horses have left on the bare slope,
The silence that grazes like two shapes where they have been.

The slow vocabulary of sleep

                   spits out its consonants
And drifts in its vowely weather,
Sun-pocked, the afternoon dying among its odors,
The cocaine smell of the wind,
The too-sweet and soft-armed

                   fragrance around the reluctant lilac bush.

Flecked in the underlap, however,

                   half-glimpsed, half-recognized,
Something unordinary persists,
Something unstill, never-sleeping, just possible past reason.
Then unflecked by evening's overflow

                   and its counter current.
What mystery can match its maliciousness, what moan?

COLLEGE DAYS

Mooresville, North Carolina, September, 1953.
Hearts made of stone, doodly wop, doodly wop, will never break . . . I
Should have paid more attention, *doodly wop, doodly wop,*
To the words and not just the music.
Stonestreet's Cafe,
                          the beginning of what might be loosely called
My life of learning and post-adolescent heartbreak-without-borders.
All I remember now is four years of Pabst Blue Ribbon beer,
A novel or two, and the myth of Dylan Thomas—
American lay-by, the academic chapel and parking lot.
O, yes, and my laundry number, 597.

What does it say about me that what I recall best
Is a laundry number—
                         that only reality endures?
Hardly. Still, it's lovely to hope so,
That speculation looms like an ever-approaching event
Darkly on the horizon,
                        and bids us take shelter,
Though like Cavafy's barbarians, does not arrive.
That's wishful thinking, Miguel,
But proper, I guess,
                        to small rooms and early morning hours,
Where juke joints and clean clothes come in as a second best.
Is sin, as I said one time, more tactile than a tree?

Some things move in and dig down

                                  whether you want them to or not.

Like pieces of small glass your body subsumes when you are young,

They exit transformed and easy-edged

Many years later, in middle age, when you least expect them,

And shine like Lot's redemption.

College is like this, a vast, exact,

                              window of stained glass

That shatters without sound as you pass,

Year after year disappearing, unnoticed and breaking off.

Gone, you think, when you are gone, thank God. But look again.

Already the glass is under your skin,

                              already the journey's on.

There is some sadness involved, but not much.

                                    Nostalgia, too, but not much.

Those years are the landscape of their own occasions, nothing lost,

It turns out, the solemn sentences metabolized

Into the truths and tacky place mats

We lay out

               when custom demands it.

That world becomes its own image, for better or worse

—The raven caws, the Weed-Eater drones—

And has no objective correlative to muscle it down.

It floats in the aether of its own content,

                              whose grass we lie on,

Listening to nothing. And to its pale half-brother, the nothingness.

NIGHT THOUGHTS UNDER A CHINA MOON

Out here, where the clouds pass without end,
One could walk in any direction till water cut the trail,
The Hunter Gracchus in his long body

                               approaching along the waves
Each time in his journey west of west.

BEDTIME STORY

The generator hums like a distant *ding an sich*.
It's early evening, and time, like the dog it is,

         is hungry for food,
And will be fed, don't doubt it, will be fed, my small one.
The forest begins to gather its silences in.
The meadow regroups and hunkers down

         for its cleft feet.

Something is wringing the rag of sunlight

         inexorably out and hanging.
Something is making the reeds bend and cover their heads.
Something is licking the shadows up,
And stringing the blank spaces along, filling them in.
Something is inching its way into our hearts,

       scratching its blue nails against the wall there.

Should we let it in?

      Should we greet it as it deserves,
Hands on our ears, mouths open?
Or should we bring it a chair to sit on, and offer it meat?
Should we turn on the radio,

        should we clap our hands and dance
The Something Dance, the welcoming Something Dance?

       I think we should, love, I think we should.

TRANSPARENCIES

Our lives, it seems, are a memory
                     we had once in another place.
Or are they its metaphor?
The trees, if trees they are, seem the same,
                         and the creeks do.
The sunlight blurts its lucidity in the same way,
And the clouds, if clouds they really are,
                      still follow us,
One after one, as they did in the old sky, in the old place.

I wanted the metaphor, if metaphor it is, to remain
                         always the same one.
I wanted the hills to be the same,
And the rivers too,
                 especially the old rivers,
The French Broad and Little Pigeon, the Holston and Tennessee,
And me beside them, under the stopped clouds and stopped stars,
I wanted to walk in that metaphor,
                      untouched by time's corruption.

I wanted the memory adamantine, never-changing.
I wanted the memory amber,
                   and me in it,
A figure among its translucent highlights and swirls,
Mid-stride in its glittery motions.
I wanted the memory cloud-sharp and river-sharp,

My place inside it transfiguring, ever-still,

                         no wind and no wave.

But memory has no memory. Or metaphor.
It moves as it wants to move,
                   and never measures the distance.
People have died of thirst in crossing a memory.
Our lives are summer cotton, it seems,
                     and good for a season.
The wind blows, the rivers run, and waves come to a head.
Memory's logo is the abyss, and that's no metaphor.

MORNING OCCURRENCE AT XANADU

Swallows are flying grief-circles over their featherless young,
Night-dropped and dead on the wooden steps.
The aspen leaves have turned gray,

                    slapped by the hard, west wind.

Someone who knows how little he knows
Is like the man who comes to a clearing in the forest,

                        and sees the light spikes,
And suddenly senses how happy his life has been.

THE SILENT GENERATION III

These are our voices, active, passive and suppressed,

         and these are our syllables.

We used them to love your daughters, we used them to love your sons.

We travelled, we stayed home, we counted our days out

        like prescription pills.

In the end, like everyone, we had too much to say.

     ————

We lived by the seat of our pants, we bet on the come

Only to come up short,

     and see, as the smoke began to clear,

The life we once thought that boundless canopy of sky,

Was just the sound of an axe, echoing in the woods.

     ————

We hadn't the heart for heartlessness,

       we hadn't the salt or the wound.

The words welled,

    but goodness and mercy declined to follow us.

We carried our wings on our own backs, we ate our dead.

Like loose light bulbs, we kept our radiance to ourselves.

     ————

Not heavy enough to be the hangman's burden,

       our noosed names

Are scrawled in the dust discursively, line after line.

Too strange for our contemporaries,

                                   we'll prove to be

Not strange enough for posterity.

———————

O you who come after us,

Read our remains,

                   study the soundless bones and do otherwise.

Saturday Morning Satori

When the mind is exalted, the body is lightened, the Chinese say,
Or one of them said,

                      and feels as though it could float in the wind.
Neglecting to say like what, I think it might be like a leaf,
Like this leaf in careless counterpoint

                                down from an unseen tree,
West wind deep bass line under raven shrill.

                          No, it's a feather,

One thing in a world of images.
It's not a question of what we think, we think too much.
It's not a question of what we say, we say too much.
A thing is not an image,

                        imagination's second best,
A language in which the heavens call out to us

                                each day in their gutterals.

Wrong Notes

To bring the night sky to life,
                           strike a wrong note from time to time,
Half for the listening ear, half for the watching eye.
Up here, just north of the Cabinet Mountains,
                                   the Great Bear
Seems closer to me than the equinox, or rinsed glints
In the creek hurrying elsewhere into evening's undergrowth.

The same way with the landscape.
                              Our meadow, for instance,
Has two creeks that cross it;
                             they join and become one about halfway down,
And that runs under my west window.
These are the flash and lapped scales
That trouble the late sunlight,
                            and spark the moon fires and moon dregs.

At other times, it seems invisible, or they do,
Moving slowly in dark slides
                         from beaver break to beaver break,
Muscling down from spruce shadow through willow shadow.
Above its margins the deer graze,
                             two coyotes skulk and jump,
And clouds start to herd together like wounded cattle.

And what does this matter?
                         Not much, unless you're one of those,

As I am, who hears a music in such things, who thinks,

When the sun goes down, or the stars do,

That the tune they're doing is his song,

That the instruments of the given world

                                        play only for him.

The Minor Art of Self-Defense

Landscape was never a subject matter, it was a technique,
A method of measure,
                                        a scaffold for structuring.
I stole its silences, I stepped to its hue and cry.

Language was always the subject matter, the idea of God
The ghost that over my little world
Hovered, my mouthpiece for meaning,
                                        my claw and bright beak . . .

THE AUTHOR

Nancy Crampton

CHARLES WRIGHT was born in 1935 in Pickwick Dam, Hardin County, Tennessee, and grew up in Tennessee and North Carolina. He attended Davidson College, The University of Iowa, and the University of Rome. From 1957–1961 he was in the Army Intelligence Service, stationed for most of this time in Verona, Italy. In 1963–65 he was a Fulbright student in Rome, translating the poems of the Italian poets Eugenio Montale and Cesare Pavese. In 1968–69 he was a Fulbright Lecturer at the University of Padua. From 1966–1983 he was a member of the English Department of the University of California, Irvine. Since 1983, he has been a Professor of English (since 1988, Souder Family Professor of English) at the University of Virginia. He has taught, in a visiting capacity, at the University of Iowa, Princeton University, and Columbia University, as well as being Distinguished Visiting Professor at the Universita' Degli Studi, Florence, Italy, spring 1992.